AKIO MORITA
AND
SONY

DAVID MARSHALL

Picture Credits

The Advertising Archives: 20 (top); **Colorific:** 20 (right) / Ben Martin, 47 (top) / Ben Martin; **Edimedia:** 30 / A. Snark; **Gamma:** 6, 8 / Kaku Kurita, 16 (bottom) / Kaku Kurita, 21 / Francis Apesteguy, 37 / Figaro Magazine, 40 / Kaku Kurita, 46 / P. Kurz, 50 / F. Reglain, 57 / Wada, 60 / Frederic Reglain; **The Grayling Company:** 24; **Horizon International Images:** 7 (top) / Adina Amsel, 13; **Hulton Deutsch Collection Limited:** 12, 17 (bottom); **Images Colour Library:** 58; **The Kobal Collection / Columbia Pictures Industries Inc.:** 54, 55; **London Features International Ltd.:** 53 (left) / Kevin Mazar, 53 (right) / Ron Wolfson, 54 / Phil Loftus; **Monatex / Exley Publications Ltd.:** 14; **Rex Features / Today:** 35; **Sony:** 4-5, 9, 17 (top), 19 (bottom), 23, 26-27 / Kohda, 28, 29, 30-31, 32 (both), 33, 38, 41, 42, 43, 44, 45, 51, 56, 59 (both); **Spectrum Colour Library:** 10 / Jean Kugler, 11 / D&J Heaton, 19 (top), 22 (both), 25, 34, 47 (bottom), 48-49; **TCL Stock Directory UK:** 18; **UPI / Bettmann:** 7 (bottom), 15.

The Publishers would like to thank Understanding Industry for its kind permission to reproduce the quotes from the fifth edition of *Understanding Industry Now* by Rosemarie Stefanou, published by Hodder and Stoughton.

The Publishers would like to thank Mr. W. H. Vestey, Sony Italia S.p.A. and Monatex for their help in the production of this book.

"Sony"; "Handycam"; "Watchman"; "Walkman"; "Trinitron"; "Data Discman"; "MiniDisc"; "JumboTron"; "Mavica"; "Betamax" and "My First Sony" are all trademarks of the Sony Corporation, Japan.

"Columbia" and "Tristar" are trademarks of Sony Music Entertainment Inc.

Published in Great Britain in 1995
by Exley Publications Ltd,
16 Chalk Hill, Watford,
Herts WD1 4BN, United Kingdom.

J 621.30752
M862
<B>

ISBN 1-85015-484-8

Series editor: Samantha Armstrong
Editorial assistants: Helen Lanz and Alison MacTier
Picture editors: Alex Goldberg and James Clift of Image Select
Typeset by Delta Print, Watford, Herts, U.K.
Printed by Kossuth Printing House Co. in Hungary.

AKIO MORITA
AND
SONY

DAVID MARSHALL

≣EXLEY

World leader

Sony Corporation was founded by two people in 1946 in a bombed-out department store in Tokyo, Japan, and grew to be the world's leading manufacturer of electronic goods in just fifty years. Sony's founders, Masaru Ibuka and Akio Morita, built it into one of the largest and most innovative companies in the world.

Sony's success was based on a fundamental principle to which all its workers subscribed – this spirit enabled them to overcome the most intricate problems. Sony's main belief was summed up in its company statement, "The road of the pioneer is full of difficulties, but in spite of many hardships, people of Sony always unite harmoniously and closely

because of their joy of participating in creative work and their pride in contributing their own unique talents to this aim."

Helping Japan recover

Akio Morita's drive for success came largely from the events happening in Japan as he grew up. World War II had dragged on in the Pacific and the United States was determined to bring it to a swift and decisive end. It used its ultimate weapon, the atomic bomb. On September 2, 1945, the Japanese army formally surrendered to the American forces.

At the time Akio Morita, a twenty-four year old university graduate, was working in Japan's capital, Tokyo, as part of a team of scientists and engineers who were trying to perfect weapons for the war effort.

Morita's reaction to defeat was that of a scientist, as well as that of a loyal Japanese citizen. He had realized many months earlier that Japan's cause was hopeless. However, he had assumed that its leaders would be determined to keep going. Besides, Japan had never lost a war in its whole history. After the atomic bombs were dropped, however, further resistance was futile. "We might as well give up our research right now," Morita said to his colleagues.

Right: Japan surrenders at the end of World War II. General MacArthur signs the surrender document on behalf of the United States and its allies on the battleship Missouri *on September 2, 1945. Japan would never have surrendered if it had not been for the atomic bomb. Japan's defeat in the war made its people absolutely determined to succeed in the peace that followed.*

"If the Americans can build an atomic bomb, we must be too far behind in every field to catch up."

This was a sad statement – and one that Akio Morita felt very strongly. Over the next few days, passing through the ruins of towns and cities, it became increasingly obvious that, if Japan were to recover from the war and build a new society, it would need all the talent it could muster.

Akio Morita began to feel that he could play an important part in this resurrection in some way. He never dreamed just how big a role this would be.

Statement of intent

From that moment Akio Morita was determined to succeed – for Japan's future and his own. Both of Sony's founders, Ibuka and Morita, had an idea and a vision of what might be possible if they applied themselves – and took calculated business risks.

At the beginning, Sony did not have a company song, unlike most Japanese organizations, but it did

Akio Morita – the man who changed the listening habits of the world. By the 1990s, he had built up a worldwide reputation among fellow engineers and senior executives for his combination of technical skill and business sense.

have a statement of intent referred to as the "Sony Spirit." It said, "Through progress, Sony wants to serve the whole world." In doing so the company would always be "a seeker of the unknown."

Ibuka and Morita wanted Sony to be a pioneering company. It would also be different from many Western businesses in its attitude to its employees: "Sony has a principle of respecting and encouraging one's ability – the right [person] in the right post – and always tries to bring out the best in a person and believes in him and constantly allows him to develop his ability," the statement of intent revealed. "This is the vital force of Sony."

Akio Morita summarized another important element of his business philosophy when he said, "[Others] look about ten minutes ahead, while Japanese look ahead ten years."

Sony Corporation has established a well-earned reputation for producing up-to-the-minute, high quality electronic products, such as this "Handycam" video camcorder.

Early years

Akio Morita was born on January 26, 1921, to Kyuzaemon and Shuko Morita of Kosugaya village, near the industrial city of Nagoya. He was born into one of Japan's oldest and best sake-brewing families. Sake, an alcoholic drink made from rice, is the Japanese national drink. It is also a Japanese cultural symbol and plays a part in many religious rituals, such as the traditional marriage ceremony.

Akio's parents consulted an old, respected scholar of Japanese and Chinese literature to find a name for their first child. "Akio" uses the Japanese character for "enlightened," pronounced "Aki." The Japanese alphabet uses Chinese characters which have many

Japan is a culturally rich society, with great traditions and long-established rituals. As Akio Morita himself wrote, "For many years, Japan has bestowed the title Living National Treasure on the best craftsmen and artists of traditional Japanese culture."

ways of being pronounced and "Akio" can also mean "uncommon." The family thought the name, coupled with Morita, which means "prosperous rice field," would give their son a good start in life.

Akio's family had been making sake for more than three hundred years. Because the business was so central to the life of the Japanese community, the Morita family always took an important role in community life as well.

Akio's father, Kyuzaemon Morita, was an excellent businessman, but the sake company was in serious financial trouble when he took it over. Akio's grandfather had not taken an active part in running the business and had employed managers to run the company. His father had the task of restoring the

Morita family fortunes. No outside manager could be counted on to do that for him. By the time Akio was born, the business was back on its feet.

Barrels of sake, Japan's national drink and cultural symbol. Akio Morita belonged to one of the oldest sake-brewing families in Japan.

Home life

Akio lived in a big, rambling house on one of the wealthiest streets in Nagoya. He grew up with his younger sister and two younger brothers, his aunt, uncle, grandparents, and six servants. There were also three or four young people living with them whom the family was helping to send through school in exchange for housework. Akio's mother, Shuko, had a full-time job in the home and was, Akio remembered, a "clever woman of great patience."

It was his mother who brought the family – and especially Akio – into the present century with changes that she made. Although she was very traditional – she always wore a kimono, for example – she was pleased to break with tradition when it was to Akio's advantage. Akio was a serious and studious boy, so she was happy to give him a room of his own with a desk. Later, she provided a second desk when he needed a workbench for his scientific experiments and a western-style bed, rather than the traditional quilted bedding on the tatami mats used by most Japanese people. As Akio observed, "I was being modernized even as a child."

Western influences

Akio's life was westernized in many ways. After living in Paris, his uncle Keizo brought stories and pictures from Europe. Akio was only eight years old and fell under the spell of discovery. He was determined to travel when he was older and enjoy this new world for himself.

His mother enjoyed western classical music and played many records on an old Victrola player. The sound of records on the old wind-up equipment was poor and Akio's father believed that it was important to have not only the best records, but the best way of playing them. He appreciated music from a technical standpoint rather than an artistic one. When new electric Victor machines became available Akio's father had to have one despite their very high cost.

The sound from the new machine was fantastic in comparison with the old one. It was with a mixture of wonder and fascination that the young Akio listened to Ravel, Mozart, Beethoven, Bach, and Brahms. He was obsessed with how a mixture of different components could be arranged, making it possible to hear the sound so well – or even at all! He became hooked on electronics to the extent that he later admitted, "I became so engrossed in my electronic tinkering that I almost flunked out of school."

Akio was always seated up at the front of the class with the other struggling pupils. Although he was good at mathematics, physics, and chemistry, his grades in geography, history, and Japanese were always below average.

Business training

Akio was given training in the family business at the earliest possible age. At eleven, he was told, "You are the boss from the start. You are the eldest son in the family. Remember that."

It was while turning the handle of an old record player for his mother, so that they could listen to recordings of Enrico Caruso, that eight year old Akio Morita first became interested in electronics and sound reproduction.

However, he learned many other important lessons about being in charge and accepting the consequences of his own actions. His father told him, "Don't think that just because you are at the top you can boss others around. Be very clear on what you have decided to do and what you ask others to do and take full responsibility for it."

Akio was also taught that chastising workers or looking to blame other people for mistakes that are not of their own making is a useless activity. He learned that in business, as in life, people have to be motivated to achieve their full potential. As he said, "Everybody wants to succeed. In learning to work with employees, I discovered, a manager needs to cultivate the traits of patience and understanding. You can't make selfish moves or get mean with people. These concepts have stayed with me and helped me develop the philosophy of management that served me very well in the past and continues to serve me and my company today."

Love for physics

Despite his low grades and his neglect of certain subjects, seventeen year old Akio Morita decided that he would try to get a place in the science department at the Eighth Higher School. This was quite an ambition for a reluctant scholar.

He put away his electronic gadgets and magazines and concentrated on his studies for a whole year.

"The value of the nation's investment in its cultural and scientific foundations depends . . . on the education of our young people; not only scientific education but also education of pupils at an early age which has its own particular importance."

Sir Paul Girolami, chairman of Glaxo Holdings plc, 1993.

Thanks to special coaching provided by his family, and his own determination, he achieved a pass. This single-mindedness was typical of Akio.

At first, high school was difficult too. It was not until his third year that he began to enjoy learning. In this year he was able to specialize, and he chose physics. "I chose physics, where I always got straight As. I was in love with physics and I idolized my instructors," Akio remembered.

One of his teachers at high school had watched Akio's obsession with physics grow and he decided

Osaka University, pictured in 1994. It has been rebuilt since the days when Akio Morita studied physics here. He was the first in fifteen generations of his family to break away from the family business.

to introduce Akio to one of the highest authorities in physics in Japan, Tsunesaburo Asada. Asada taught at the most important university for young scientists, the Osaka Imperial University. It also had the most modern facilities in Japan. As far as Akio was concerned, it was ideal.

Akio's father was disappointed that his son had chosen to go to university to study physics and not something that would help the family business, like economics. He did not try to change Akio's mind, but he still assumed that his son would give up his "hobby" of electronics and take his rightful place at the head of the family business.

Osaka University

When Akio, aged nineteen, arrived at university, it was 1940 and World War II had just begun. Most of Professor Asada's laboratories and time were occupied with research to help the Japanese war effort. Akio helped too. Not long after his arrival,

Akio was faced with a difficult choice. He could either enter the Japanese navy for a short time and become a technical officer, or he could join the navy for life and immediately be sent to carry out research at his own university.

The problem with the first choice was that he could be sent to a ship in charge of radar, but not far from the front line, and from there probably into the full war machine. The problem with the second option was that he could see himself being in the navy for a very long time – which was not what he wanted. After some thought Akio decided on the second choice because he could see it would give him the possibility of being back in the university, doing research. And that was exactly what happened.

Akio finished his second year at university. However, the war intensified and, like everyone else in the country, all physics students were put under direct military control. This meant that he was sent to work not in a laboratory, but in a factory. For several

When the Japanese air force attacked the U.S. Pacific naval base, Pearl Harbor, on December 7, 1941, it brought the United States into World War II, and eventually led to the Japanese defeat.

weeks he had to put up with the drudgery of using a metal file in a machine shop, making steel parts for Japanese planes. Eventually he was transferred to an optics laboratory to carry out research into aerial photography. This production line experience stayed with him for the rest of his life – he never forgot what it felt like to work on a factory floor doing a repetitive manual task.

Special projects with Ibuka

Soon Akio Morita joined a special project group composed of researchers from the army, navy, and civilian sectors. They were all working on heat-seeking devices. One of the most brilliant researchers was an electronics engineer named Masaru Ibuka.

Masaru Ibuka was thirteen years older than Akio – but became his closest friend and collaborator. Although Akio was younger than anyone else on the team, he was given the same chances and respect as all the others. Because of the training his father had given him in the family business, Akio was able to hold his own in this high-ranking company, despite his youth.

A challenge is set

As the war came to an end Akio's future looked uncertain. At one point it looked as though the Japanese High Command might even order them all to commit suicide rather than let their ideas be taken over by the enemy. The Japanese emperor, Hirohito, made an announcement on the radio that struck Akio deeply. The emperor was held in extremely high esteem by the Japanese people. For instance, ordinary people were not even allowed to look at him; if he was passing by train or by car, people along the route were required to face away. It was a moment for the history books when the emperor spoke to the nation on the radio for the first time.

He said that the Japanese people could "pave the way for a grand peace for all generations to come," but they had to do it "by enduring the unendurable and suffering what is insufferable." He urged Japan to look ahead. "Unite your total strength to be

Emperor Hirohito rejected the idea that he was a divine leader and accepted a new form of democratic government that took away much of his power in Japan.

devoted to the construction for the future," he said. And he challenged the nation to "keep pace with the progress of the world."

It was a challenge that Akio Morita in particular was to meet willingly.

Into business

In 1946, after long consultations, Akio Morita and Masaru Ibuka decided to go into business together. They wanted to form an electronics company and use their expertise gathered during the war, and also point the way for future businesses.

The company they founded was named Tokyo Tsushin Kogyo Kabushiki Kaisha which translates into English as Tokyo Telecommunications Engineering Company. The present name of Sony Corporation was not adopted until 1958.

For Akio's family, taking the eldest son out of the family business was a serious matter. The new business proposal had to be discussed with Akio's father. To Akio's surprise and relief, his father agreed at once. His younger brother, Kazuaki, was willing to take over the family business at the appropriate time.

The first factory

In January 1947, when Akio was twenty-six, the company moved into a dilapidated, very cheap, old warehouse in Tokyo. It had holes in the roof and was surrounded by war damage, but it was their base.

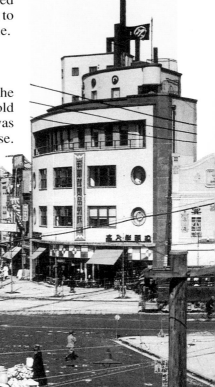

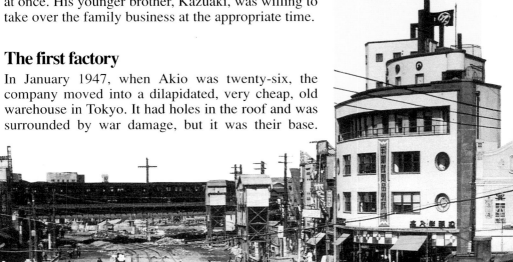

A modern television control room. Thanks to the latest technology, such as Sony's broadcasting equipment, one person can control the sound and pictures that are transmitted to millions of people.

Originally the company made voltmeters, electrically heated cushions, resonator sound generators for the telegraphic industry, and other products in this field.

Ibuka and Morita managed to acquire a small, well-used truck for transportation. They then discovered that they alone, the two top executives of the company, were able to drive. This meant that on a typical day they would do their "executive" work, researching and planning, along with the manual work of loading deliveries, driving the truck, and delivering products. A full day – and one that showed what running a small business was truly all about.

Ibuka was determined to make a new product that would establish the company at the forefront of the electronics business. The American occupying forces had taken over the major Japanese public broadcasting unit, NHK, and needed new technical equipment such as mixing units and studio systems. Ibuka put in a bid to build a large broadcasting mixing unit for NHK.

Thanks to a friend who was in charge of engineering reconstruction at NHK, the Americans were persuaded to accept the bid from Ibuka. The American general who came to inspect Morita's factory could not understand why this outfit, in such a small, rundown building, should get the contract. In spite of his misgivings, the contract was signed, but Morita and Ibuka were advised to place buckets of sand and water all over the building to stop it from going up in smoke while they were working!

When the new equipment was delivered to NHK, its quality was excellent and it was delivered on time. Although the factory wasn't very attractive, it produced reliable, high-quality goods. Ibuka's and Morita's reputation was beginning to be established. They had shown that they could be trusted – that they never let a customer down.

First tape recorder

Despite this success, Tokyo Tsushin Kogyo was still far away from producing the breakthrough item it needed. But, while delivering the equipment to NHK, Ibuka had seen the latest American invention

– the Wilcox-Gay tape recorder. It was the first tape recorder he had seen and it fascinated him. Ibuka spent a few minutes examining it and decided that this was the type of device that he wanted their company to produce. After a great deal of persuasion, the American officer who owned the machine agreed to let Ibuka borrow it so that he could take it back to the factory and show the others.

Without any real hesitation, the team decided that not only would they try to make tape recorders, but also the tape to use on the machine. They reasoned that having bought a tape recorder, customers would also need to buy tapes. This would give the company a market for its tapes for the foreseeable future.

So Tokyo Tsushin Kogyo's first major consumer item was an audio tape recorder, introduced in Japan in 1950. Akio Morita was thrilled, believing this to be the company's big breakthrough product. But there was a problem. "We were in for a rude awakening. The tape recorder was so new to Japan that almost no one knew what a tape recorder was,

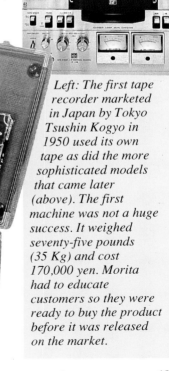

Left: The first tape recorder marketed in Japan by Tokyo Tsushin Kogyo in 1950 used its own tape as did the more sophisticated models that came later (above). The first machine was not a huge success. It weighed seventy-five pounds (35 Kg) and cost 170,000 yen. Morita had to educate customers so they were ready to buy the product before it was released on the market.

a SONY portable designed expressly for your car

SONY

Above: By 1963 Sony was able to offer the most modern and sophisticated in-car radio – which could also be taken out and used away from the car whenever required. Portability of sound was always a fascination of Akio Morita's and a mark of Sony products.

Right: Akihabara electronic market in Tokyo, just one of a huge number of markets where it is possible to buy any electronic goods. Companies like Sony helped to create a popular demand for such goods in Japan.

and most of the people who did know could not see why they should buy one. It was not something people felt they needed. We could not sell it."

Find a market

At the start of their business careers, Morita and Ibuka had learned a very important lesson. There was no point in having perfected a great product if there was no market for it.

The tape recorder was very heavy and expensive. Morita admitted, "I then realized that having unique

technology and being able to make unique products are not enough to keep a business going. You have to be able to sell the products, and to do that you have to show the potential buyer the real value of what you are selling." He also realized that he was going to have to be the salesman for the company.

With further research and many improvements, the tape recorder's mechanism was made smaller and more attractive. Now it was bigger than a briefcase, but smaller than a small suitcase. It was known as the H-type recorder.

New systems

The company's next step was to keep on top of new technology in its field. In 1949 a new high frequency broadcasting transmission system had become available for purchase in Japan – and Morita and Ibuka had only enough money to buy half of it. The other half was bought up by another Japanese electronics company. This system, known as AC-Bias, produced a recording with much less noise and distortion than had ever been possible before.

Morita informed every other company in Japan and those all over the world that if they wished to use the system in Japan, they would have to buy the right to do so from Tokyo Tsushin Kogyo. Very few companies were interested, but those that were paid for the privilege. Morita could see that the company now had a steady source of income for the future.

This brought them their next business experience. Morita and Ibuka learned that a company in the United States was using the system – and breaking Tokyo Tsushin Kogyo's ownership rights by exporting into Japan. Morita was prepared to take the American company to court, despite the financial cost involved.

The dispute taught Morita a great deal, especially the importance of patience at such times. It took five years for Morita to win his case. Any equipment sold in Japan that used this AC-Bias system then had to pay a royalty to his company.

Akio and Yoshiko Morita – a hugely successful partnership. Akio Morita relied on his wife's ability as an "unofficial international diplomat," and her personality and determination to succeed when the family moved to the United States in 1964.

The family man

When Akio Morita was thirty he was introduced to and married Yoshiko Kamei. Yoshiko came from a distinguished Tokyo family involved in bookselling and publishing. As a child, Yoshiko's life had been very similar to Akio's. She and Akio were immediately attracted to one another.

Their Tokyo household was always bustling and there was constant business talk. For more than forty years, Yoshiko was Akio's permanent front line assistant. As he himself affirmed, "I had left her alone a great deal in Tokyo during my business travels, and she ... acted as my confidante and business liaison when I was out of town. I would often call her with news and messages to be delivered at the office and elsewhere, and I frequently consulted with her."

In 1952, the Moritas had their first son, Hideo. Two more children followed: a second son, Masao, in 1954 and, in 1956, a daughter, Naoko.

World markets

By now Morita and Ibuka could see that if they were going to be really successful, they would have to travel the world selling their products and finding out about the latest advances in the field of electronics.

While on a visit to the United States selling their successful and well-established tape recorders, Masaru Ibuka learned about a new invention that would transform the electronics industry, the transistor. Transistors are used to amplify electronic signals, but their main advantage was that they were much smaller than the bulky vacuum tubes then in use. The changes the transistor could bring were huge.

Miniaturization has always appealed to the Japanese – Japanese boxes have been made to fit into each other, fans to fold, art to roll into neat scrolls.

Bonsai trees are deliberately kept small, reflecting the Japanese love of miniaturization. The Imperial Japanese collection of bonsai trees includes examples that are over three hundred years old.

Screens depicting an entire city can be folded and tucked neatly away. At this time, however, the world trend was for sound reproduction systems to be made as big as possible. The theory was that the more accessories, the better the sound reproduction.

Contrary to this trend, Morita and Ibuka were determined to work with transistors and to make their equipment as small as possible. Morita went to

New York in 1953 to buy the right to use transistors. The possibilities for the future of their company were now fully in place.

Name change

It was during an overseas visit, that Morita realized that Tokyo Tsushin Kogyo Kabushiki Kaisha was not an effective company name.

Even in translation, the English name – Tokyo Telecommunications Engineering Company – was too clumsy. Morita decided not only that they should have a new company name, but that it should also be a brand new name. He had noticed that many big companies in the United States had three-letter logos – ABC, NBC, RCA, and AT&T. It was time for them to change to something much smaller.

Ibuka and Morita took a long time to decide on the new name. While thumbing through a dictionary, they came across the Latin word *sonus,* meaning sound. They also knew that bright young men in Japan at the time were known as "sonny" or "sonny boys" by the occupying American troops. They decided that all they needed to do was to drop one of the letters and they would have the perfect name – and so the company was given a new name, Sony.

The word meant nothing at all – in any language. This was an important point when another company tried to ride to success on the back of the Sony name.

"We got the patent licence for the transistor in 1953, but it took more than ten years to make this transistor into a big business for us. So for ten years we invested with patience and confidence."

Akio Morita.

Sony's "Handycam" and video printer gives anyone the opportunity to record and playback what they see or even print copies of their chosen images.

It claimed that the word "sony" was in such common usage that it was in the public domain and could therefore be used by anyone, for anything. When challenged by Sony's lawyers, however, they could not find a single instance of the word in any dictionary, in any language.

Branding

Akio Morita carried on gaining access to new overseas technology – the microchip, the audio cassette from Europe, and the video recorder from the United States.

In 1955 Sony's first transistor radio was sold and, two years later, the first tiny "pocketable" radio was introduced. At the time, it was by far the world's smallest radio, but it was still slightly too big to go into a normal shirt pocket. In order to convince potential customers that it could be carried in this way, Sony had a range of new shirts produced with extra large pockets!

During the 1950s, Akio Morita found it disheartening to see how little respect Japanese goods were given outside Japan. Most people

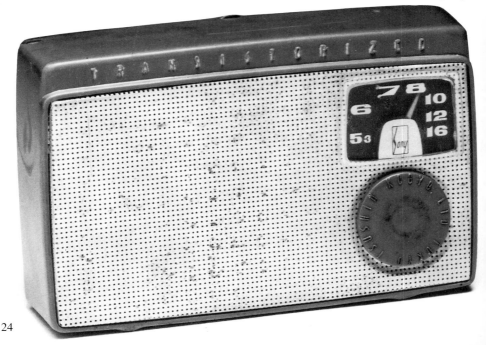

associated Japan with cheap plastic toys. In choosing Sony's name they had not deliberately set out to hide their country's name – but it certainly helped.

In international trading law it was essential that the country of origin be stamped on products. Sony printed the line "Made in Japan" as small as possible. On at least one occasion United States Customs thought it was printed too small and made Sony put it on again in larger print.

To deal with this negative reputation, Morita soon learned that he was going to have to educate the public. In his own words, "marketing is a form of communication," and he was going to have to market not only his products, but also his country.

Traditional Japanese methods of selling kept product manufacturers out of the way of the customer, so this was a new approach for a Japanese

company. Also, Sony was making products that no one had ever seen before. It became apparent that in order to sell its products, Sony would have to educate the public to want them.

A big order and a big problem

As a marketing man, Akio Morita found great success. But in 1957, he had two experiences that shaped a great deal of his and Sony's thinking for the next thirty years. He was trying to sell the first small transistor radio to anyone who would buy it. While on a sales trip in the United States, he went to meet with the executives of a large electrical product manufacturer, Bulova.

Bulova really liked Sony's little radio and ordered one hundred thousand of them. This was a staggeringly big order for Sony. The only thing Bulova insisted on was that the radios be sold under its own name. Akio Morita, from a fairly small, recently established Japanese company, turned the offer down. He had too much pride in the work and expertise that had gone into perfecting the radio to allow it to be sold under another company's name.

Morita made a rule – in order to establish its own reputation, Sony would not agree to supply

"Mr. Morita, it turns out, is not an inventor, but a salesman of technology. His dreams are about selling a million Walkman portable compact-disc players, not about making them. His aim, he says, is to bring consumer products to people. Often the hardest task is not developing an innovation, but in demonstrating to people why they might want it."

Stefan Wagstyl,
the Financial Times, 1988.

Left: Inside the Sony Kohda factory, an automatic, or robotic, assembly line makes video equipment. Automatic assembly lines are widely used by manufacturers like Sony for maximum precision and efficiency of production.

other companies with its products. If it researched and produced a new machine, it was for Sony to market entirely by itself.

While full of admiration for Morita's resolve, some of the Sony executives and workers were fearful of turning down an order such as the Bulova one. Morita continued his rounds of the major companies in the United States and came across a large retail outlet with over 150 stores across the country. The American buyer liked the radios and asked Morita to prepare a price quotation on quantities of five thousand, ten thousand, thirty thousand, fifty thousand, and one hundred thousand radios. What was more, they would be sold with the Sony name on them. Here was the perfect opportunity for Morita to recover from turning down the Bulova order.

Balancing costs

In his hotel room that night, Morita sat down and worked out a price for each radio. He soon realized that the usual business idea of "the higher the quantity ordered, the lower the price" would not work for Sony in this instance.

The company had moved to bigger premises close

> *"Technology is no obstacle: only cost and imagination."*
> Steven Butler,
> *the* Financial Times, *1991.*

The transistor led to the invention of the silicon chip, the semiconductor and the circuit board. If these complex and sophisticated pieces of equipment are to work properly, they must be absolutely perfect. This is the "clean room" at the Sony semiconductor factory at Oita, Japan, where every possible precaution is taken to guarantee purity.

to, but better than, the bombed-out shell it had first used. Even so, Morita figured out that the factory had a capacity to make only around ten thousand radios a month. This might not even leave the capacity to make all the other items on which Sony was working. If it received an order for one hundred thousand radios a year, it would have to rent or buy bigger premises, take on more workers who would need to be trained, and generally expand.

He realized that if Sony received an order for one hundred thousand and expanded accordingly, it would be in serious trouble if a repeat order was not placed the next year. He decided that if it received a really big order, then all the additional facilities it required would have to be paid for by that order itself within that first year. At least that way Sony would not have to worry about what to do with all the surplus workers if the next order did not appear.

In Japan, companies like Sony did not just hire people and fire them whenever the orders went up or down. Sony had a long-term commitment to its employees and they, in turn, had a long-term commitment to the company.

At the right price!

With this in mind, Morita prepared his quotations for the chain store buyer. If the order was for five thousand then it would be the regular price. If it was

for ten thousand then there would be a discount. If the order was as big as thirty thousand then the price would begin to go back up again. If the order was fifty thousand then each unit would be back over the five thousand price. For one hundred thousand, the unit price would have to be much more for each radio than the five thousand price.

The buyer could hardly believe his eyes. As he said to Morita, "Mr. Morita, I have been working as a purchasing agent for nearly thirty years, and you are the first person who has ever come in here and told me that the more I buy the higher the unit price will be. It's illogical!"

Morita explained how he had arrived at the price structure, and the buyer listened carefully. After a few seconds he smiled and ordered ten thousand radios – just right for him and just right for Sony!

In 1994 the Sony flag flew alongside the national flag in over thirty countries of the world. Sony's belief in "global localization," or producing goods in the countries where they are sold, made it one of the first Japanese companies to be established in Europe. A huge investment followed there, as well as in the United States.

Sony U.S.A.

It was becoming obvious that in order for Sony to fully succeed in the United States it would have to have a separate establishment there. Morita was having to split his time between the United States and Tokyo and, as a result, the operation in the United States was suffering.

In 1960 Sony made the decision to form the Sony Corporation of America, and it was completed in 1961. The same year, Sony was faced with its first and only serious strike threat from some of its more powerful unions.

The strike was on the fifteenth anniversary of its founding and could have brought the whole organization to a halt, which would have embarrassed the company. However, Morita and his colleagues were able to defeat the strike due to their good relationship with their employees. This is a perfect illustration of the way that industry works in Japan. As Morita said, "Those companies that are most successful in Japan are those that have managed to create a shared sense of fate among all employees. . . . In the long run, your business and its future are in the hands of the people you hire."

All Morita did was point out to all the employees what Sony meant to him, and should mean to them. He

simply pledged himself, and the rest of the management, to continue to work for the good of everyone. The strike fizzled out with no further episode.

Unions

Sony had no time for "closed shops" within unions. A "closed shop" is a factory in which union leaders insist that all the workers belong to the same union. Morita claimed that this was against the rights of the individual saying that, "if people want to form another union, they have the right to do it. That is freedom and that is democracy."

Morita went on to say that, wherever they were in the world, the senior managers dealt with all their employees as members of the Sony family. Akio Morita himself visited small Sony shops, offices, and factories all over the world to talk to members of his "family." He did not do this to catch them out or to spy on them – in fact, the opposite. He wanted to show they were part of the same team and that the contribution they made was valuable.

"Teamwork and cooperation as well as friendly and constructive relationships between all members are encouraged and lead to what is known as 'the Sony Family.'"
From Sony and the New Europe.

This type of business philosophy and organization was not uncommon in Japan – but it was very different from the way organizations were run in other parts of the world.

Pioneers

At this time Sony introduced an eight-inch (20cm) transistorized television set and, in doing so, created a new market for the television. Later, the company made black and white television a thing of the past with its new "Trinitron" TV sets. Akio was always willing to commit the company to new ventures.

Sony was adventurous and realized that to continue to succeed it would have to continue to be first in new areas. Rivals would wait to see what Sony was bringing out and see if it was successful before producing their own versions.

Sony was first in the development of most major products. It built the first solid-state radios and transistorized television sets and the first portable stereo player, the "Walkman." It went on to create the "Watchman" – a hand-held television – and the "Discman" – a portable compact-disc player.

The pioneering spirit of Sony has kept it ahead of most of its rivals. Not content simply to settle for success alone, it has always tried to match its products with the life style of the times. Having developed the technology to create a portable television, it was only a matter of time before Sony produced the ultimate in transistorized television sets – the "Watchman."

Later innovations included the 3.5 inch (9cm) computer floppy disk, which had the highest storage capacity in the world for its size. Its hand-held video cameras and small videotape players also made news reporting on location easier. Sony also developed a camera that did not require film.

Research and development

This was quite a track record, and all because the company had been formed by two men for whom the world of physics and invention was as important as selling their products. As Akio Morita said, "Our plan is to lead the public with new products rather than ask them what kind of products they want. The public does not know what is possible, but we do. So instead of doing a lot of market research, we refine our thinking on a product and its use and try to create a market for it by educating and communicating with the public."

In order to do this, Sony needed to have a base for new ideas. From the beginning, Sony saw research and development – or "R & D," as it is known – as an integral part of its company plan. By the 1990s

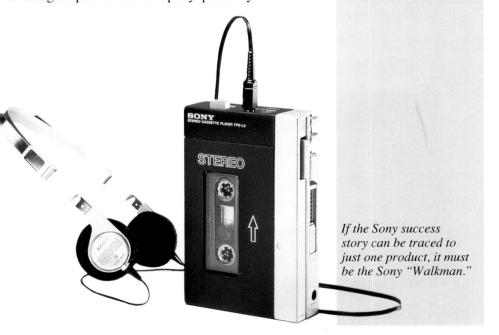

If the Sony success story can be traced to just one product, it must be the Sony "Walkman."

it would employ approximately nine thousand engineers and scientists who, between them, would create up to one thousand new products a year.

Investment

To get to this stage, Sony had to invest a lot of money in research. Part of the company slogan, "We shall create our unique products. . . . Research makes the difference," has been vital in putting Sony among the most consistently innovative companies in the world. The first step that Sony took to meet its aim was to recruit the best scientists and technicians. It then had to make the best facilities available too.

Akio also felt sure that scientific research had to be combined with practical application of that information. "Basic scientific research provides us with information which, though previously unknown, only offers hints at the future," he said. Sony used the scientific information discovered by R & D and turned it into products to sell, to make life more efficient and convenient. Sony required its development teams all around the world to be aware of the company philosophy of using information for practical purposes. "What difference does it make how fantastic and innovative your new technology is, if you do not have the ability to design a useful, attractive, 'user-friendly' product?" Morita asked.

Sony has always aimed to be the biggest and best electronics company in the marketplace. The large-screen display system, "JumboTron," is a more recent area of worldwide business for the company. In 1992 it was used to display the drama of the Summer Olympic Games in Barcelona, Spain.

Innovation

The pressure within Sony to be innovative and forward-looking has always been huge. The goals that the researchers have to achieve are established by the top level of management. Sony took the unusual step of encouraging its engineers to work in different areas of technology from those that they had studied. This meant that they could choose a project from any area in which the company was involved.

The spirit of innovation, however, has always been encouraged at all levels of the company, not just from those at the top. From the early days, Sony scientists have been as likely to consider ideas that came from workers on the factory floor as well as those from management levels. Similarly, the Sony marketing teams have always been encouraged to put forward customer feedback on the products for the R & D teams to work on.

Careful monitoring

The amount of money and commitment that Sony started to put into R & D was immense and meant that careful control and monitoring were necessary. The company invested large amounts of money in

A personal organizer is no match for Sony's "Data Discman." It has been claimed to be the most up-to-date way of keeping information at hand.

R & D and by 1993, about 232.2 billion yen ($2 billion) was being spent on it. It had four major R & D units in Japan as well as R & D units in the United Kingdom, Germany, Singapore, Australia, and the United States. In addition to these, each product division had its own scheme to develop ideas for its own market. The R & D group became one of the most important divisions in the company.

The activities of the R & D group, which worked directly under top management, were watched by the company worldwide. If some research seemed to be slow, inappropriate for a particular location, or if two locations were doing the same work, then money was being wasted. Every month, management would make a decision to combine groups, switch the research to another group, or abandon the line of research altogether. Alternatively, more money and personnel might be devoted to an area of research that was looking particularly slow.

Price of success

Revolutionary products such as the "Walkman" do not come along very often. With Sony's commitment to new products, many areas in the electronics field seemed fully developed very quickly. By 1992, 80% of Japan's households had a video recorder, 61% a stereo system, and 42% a compact-disc player. So, many of the product developments came from customer feedback on existing items. Any problems encountered by the user were analyzed and adjustments made so that the product became as perfect as possible.

Each individual Sony product would undergo tough tests before going into retail outlets. For example, before a new television model was launched it might be placed in a freezer for two days and kept at a temperature of -10°C (15°F). Then it could be put in an oven at 50°C (125°F), left switched on for the equivalent of fifteen years' use, or crashed onto a concrete floor to test its stability. The end result of these vigorous tests was an excellent reputation for quality. The investment in researching, developing, and following up R & D with such extreme tests for

*"The pace of innovation
in today's marketplace is
such that it has become
vital for firms to invest
heavily in research and
development in order to
maintain their competitive
edge. Firms which do not
accord R & D a central
role in their operations
have effectively made a
decision not to be in
business in ten or fifteen
years' time."*

Rosemarie Stefanou, from
Understanding Industry Now.

quality has proved to be worthwhile to Sony because of the reputation the company has built up with the customer. If a customer owns a Sony television that is good quality, the next electronic product that he or she purchases is more likely to be made by Sony than one of its competitors.

In its early days, Sony had the market for a new product all to itself for several months – or even years – while its rivals waited to see the market's response. This meant that Sony made a lot of money. However, as Sony's reputation grew, the time gap grew shorter and shorter before competitors started producing the same types of product and competing in the marketplace. Sometimes a high price can be paid for success.

Showrooms

In 1960 Sony opened a showroom in the Ginza district of Tokyo where people could go and try out new products before buying them, free from the attention of sales staff. It proved to be a huge commercial success.

In 1962 Morita decided that there should be

Innovation is important to Sony in both its technological progress and its marketing prowess. The company displayed its selling techniques at Live '94, a consumer products exhibition in London, with its TV tunnel promotion of the "MiniDisc."

another showroom, but this time it should be in New York. It did not take him long to realize that it had to be on the most prestigious street in New York – Fifth Avenue. Most of the stores there had their country's flag flying outside them, but the Japanese flag was not there. Akio Morita pledged that when Sony opened its store on Fifth Avenue it would also be the first to fly the Japanese flag.

In order to achieve this and all his other ambitions for Sony's expansion, Morita felt that he had to move to the United States permanently. It was during the launch of the Sony store on Fifth Avenue in October 1962 – Akio had designed and planned the interior himself – that he announced to his wife, Yoshiko, that they would be moving to New York.

No problem

Yoshiko, along with almost everyone else, had so much faith in Akio Morita's judgment that she accepted this decision without argument. This showed how far he, and Sony, had come from their humble beginnings.

In order to make sure that he kept a grip on the affairs of the whole company, Morita agreed that he would fly back to Tokyo every two months and spend at least a week there.

The decision to move to the United States was not one that came easily to Morita because he knew what an upheaval it would be for his family. When this move was contemplated his children were still young – Hideo was ten, Masao was eight, and Naoko just six. Both Akio and Yoshiko thought that, in the long term, the experience would be good for them. It was Yoshiko who made the change work so well, although she spoke practically no English.

The move took place in 1964. Akio believed that the whole family needed to move completely and without hesitation. To this end he and Yoshiko immediately sent the children to summer camp. Hideo and Masao were the only Japanese boys in the camp. They knew no English. In order to get by, they copied what the other children were doing and hoped for the best, but they were very homesick.

"Once the decision has been taken to launch a new product, it is vitally important that the development time ... between initial design and full production is reduced as much as possible. If companies take too long to introduce a product, competitors will enter the market with similar products and erode potential profits."

Rosemarie Stefanou, from
Understanding Industry Now.

When they had settled, Yoshiko took her American driving test. Because she was worried about her lack of English, she memorized all the test material, including the one hundred possible test questions, although she didn't understand much of it. She passed the whole test with a perfect score.

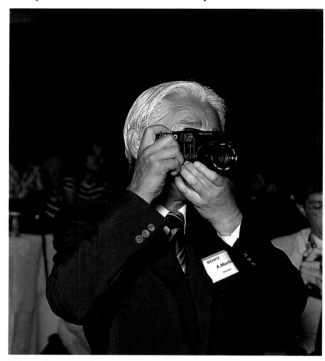

Not always in the lead

Not everything that Sony, and Morita, developed was a success. The company was one of the first to begin manufacturing calculators, but it had not counted on so many other manufacturers joining the market with their own versions. After two or three years, Sony management decided that the market was too small to sustain all the companies that were now making and marketing calculators. Sony pulled out.

Just a few years later the company saw its mistake. The problem was that when Sony began to organize its role in the huge computer business it did not have many existing resources – it had no factories or machines and little expertise to draw on.

If it had continued to make calculators this would not have been a problem. For once Sony had failed to see the long term consequences when considering the short term difficulties.

Sony was one of the first companies to recognize the potential of the videotape market. But its "Betamax" video cassette system, launched in 1975, was only a limited success because of the impact on the market of the rival VHS system.

The "Betamax" story taught Sony an important lesson and reinforced its commitment to researching and carefully developing all its products. This kind

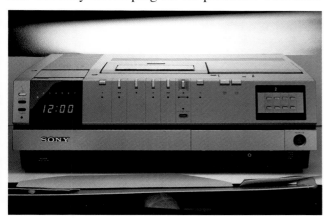

The first video cassette recorder, or VCR, was a huge engineering success – but a financial failure. Akio Morita put all his own energy behind promoting the "Betamax" VCR. As he said, "With the VCR, television is like a magazine – you can control your own schedule." Unfortunately, the rival VHS system became the market leader. The Sony system is still used by the movie and video industries, but is hardly ever seen in everyday use in the home.

of work can take years to come to fruition, however, and once research on an idea has begun products can take more than ten years to emerge.

International

When the time came to consider opening factories in other parts of the world, Sony weighed up all the options and looked at a great many locations. In the United Kingdom, it finally decided on Wales because it offered a good environment, it was convenient and low-priced, and was well served by transportation and other facilities.

The Sony showroom in Paris was opened on the Champs Élysées in 1971. By then Sony was already established as Sony Hawaii, Sony Panama, and Sony U.K. It had also negotiated a deal with CBS

Sony's "Trinitron" TV plant in Bridgend, Wales, in the United Kingdom. By the 1990s, over 55% of Sony's staff was employed outside Japan.

records in the United States to establish a joint venture in Japan. Sony had become truly international.

Keep growing

Morita had learned that, in order to continue to succeed, a business must grow – it cannot stand still. If it is not expanding then it will be declining. It was at this time that Sony set up the first manufacturing plant in the United States. It had become more and more obvious that this would happen as most of Sony's large television sets were sold in the States.

The largest part of these sets is the big picture tube – a large glass envelope containing a vacuum. The tubes made up almost all the volume of cargo being shipped to the States and were therefore expensive. It made more sense to make the tubes in the country itself rather than ship them there. Sony decided to make its products from parts bought in the countries where it already had factories established. For this reason most of Sony's television sets were made in the United States – unlike many American sets which were often made by suppliers in the Far East and shipped over to the United States.

Local business

From this point on, Sony Corporation adopted a policy of "manufacturing where the market is." This led to the growth of Sony manufacturing bases all over the world, with the intention that Sony should be able to produce as much of its business locally as it could. "Trinitron" televisions were made in Wales,

Following Sony's aim to achieve the highest possible "local content" in its products, "Trinitron" televisions were produced in three European locations including the United Kingdom. In 1994, over 40% of Sony products sold in Europe were also produced there.

Barcelona, and Germany. Audio and video equipment was made in France, and audiotape cassettes and other electronic devices were made in Italy and France. Video cassettes were also manufactured in France, and optical discs were made in Austria. By 1994 around 40% of Sony's products sold in Europe were produced locally.

Where do ideas come from?

Ideas for the growth of Sony's product base came from all sorts of different avenues. The Sony "Walkman," for example, started in the Morita household. One day, Akio's daughter, Naoko, came home from a trip and immediately ran upstairs to put a cassette into her stereo and listen to the tape.

Akio was struck by how important it was for Naoko to have music around her. He also noticed that many young people were carrying large tape players or radios on their shoulders as they walked through the streets so that they could listen to music wherever they went. The idea of a truly portable player began to obsess him. One day Ibuka walked into his office and complained about the weight of one of Sony's supposedly "portable" stereo tape recorders and its standard size headphones. Ibuka said, "I like to listen to music, but I don't want to disturb others. I can't sit there by my stereo all day. This is my solution – I take the music with me. But it's too heavy."

Problem solving

This was just the sort of electronic challenge that Akio Morita loved. He could see that if he solved Ibuka's problem, the possibilities for expanding the basic idea of a personal sound stereo were huge. He ordered some of the engineers to take one of the reliable, small tape recorders and strip out the recording circuit and speaker and replace them with a stereo amplifier. He outlined the details of what else he wanted, particularly the specification of some lightweight headphones – these proved to be the most difficult part of the project.

To his astonishment no one else seemed to like the idea. One of the engineers at the product planning meetings said, "It sounds like a good idea, but will

Sony was quick to adapt its products to capture niches in the market. "My First Sony" products were made using the wealth of technological experience that went into all Sony products – but they were packaged in a way that was appealing to the younger age group.

people buy it if it doesn't have recording capability? I don't think so." Morita stuck by his idea.

He was proved right – but not without a struggle. Morita acknowledged that his colleagues had no faith in his idea for the "Walkman" throughout the project, but, "When I pulled my bluff on the 'Walkman,' threatening to resign, my colleagues knew that I was ahead of them, that I was using all of my experience and knowledge of marketing and consumer psychology in making my decision. And because of it they [gave] themselves 100% to helping make the project a success."

This ability to bury their own feelings and follow through another's idea for the good of the company, was typical of the Sony workers' way of operating.

Stow Away or "Walkman"

It was only over the name itself that Morita may have been wrong. While he was away on a trip some young people in the company chose the name. They had all the advertising material prepared and printed with the name "Walkman" before he got back. When he returned he tried to get the name changed to something "more grammatical," but it was too late. In Japan, it was the "Walkman." However, in the United Kingdom and the United States, the Sony sales force thought that they would struggle to get the product launched with this name. Others were tried – the Stow Away and the Sound About. Neither name caught on.

It was only a few weeks later that Morita himself reluctantly rang up the sales teams and ordered them all to use the name "Walkman." It was a wise business decision: the name became firmly fixed in the customers' minds and the product became a market leader. The success of the Sony "Walkman" marked the start of a policy to always give Sony products a unique name. This policy worked on two fronts: one, the original name established the new product in the customer's mind, and two, the unique names become associated with Sony and so branded by quality. Shortly after its launch, the Sony factories could not keep up with demand for "Walkman" personal stereos.

The range of "My First Sony" products includes a number of different electronic goods from the "Walkman" to CD players, so children have a wide choice of products too.

Refining the idea

On Morita's insistence Sony had produced a set of headphones and shared leads so that people could listen to their "Walkman" with friends. This idea came to him when he realized how antisocial it could be to listen to music shut off from the world.

He noticed that the experimental model he had been listening to had annoyed his wife. She felt excluded. In order to be able to talk to his golf partner, Morita had the "Walkman" fitted with a button-activated microphone that allowed them to communicate on a "hot line." It was with surprise that he learned that both the shared leads and the "hot line" were unnecessary. People wanted to listen privately to their own music – and the Sony "Walkman" made it possible.

The Sony "Walkman" story was a perfect illustration of the efficiency of Sony and its ability to achieve great success. When the company was established, Ibuka had written a short prospectus in which he had outlined where he thought the company would go and in particular the philosophy that he and Akio Morita shared for running Sony. He concluded by saying, "If it were possible to establish conditions

The "Walkman" monument in Vienna. The invention of this piece of electronic equipment made Akio Morita a more public figure than almost any other Japanese industrialist.

where persons could become united with a firm spirit of teamwork, and exercise to their hearts' desire their technological capacity, then such an organization could bring untold pleasure and untold benefits."

Quite possibly the invention of the Sony "Walkman," and the technical possibilities it highlighted for the company, was the greatest testament to the success of that philosophy.

Investing in people

Sony, like other Japanese companies, did not invest huge sums of money in the appearance of its headquarters or company buildings.

It had new and impressive buildings around the world, but its headquarters in Tokyo were nothing more than a converted factory building. It was made comfortable and functional – but visitors still had to climb two short flights of stairs to get to the reception desk.

Generally, in Japanese industry, the investment goes into those things that relate directly to the products that are being made. Very often the company offices and factory buildings look like warehouses from the outside. Inside they are sensible and contain everything essential that the workers can possibly need. But money is not wasted on unnecessary show.

Above: Exercising and relaxing are seen as essential for all business people in Japan and playing golf is no exception. Akio Morita enjoyed playing golf for most of his professional life.

Left: Office workers take the opportunity to relax in Shinjuku Garden Park. Sony has always placed a high value on creating a good working environment for its employees. It keeps to the same principles of management worldwide, making necessary adjustments to reflect regional differences in cultures, laws, and practices, such as the number of working hours in the day.

Personnel

What Sony did invest in was personnel. The business was based on having the right people in the right places. Sony made a great commitment to recruitment. Every year Morita himself addressed the new graduate recruits in its headquarters in Tokyo. In 1986 he told the new employees to be aware that working in a company like Sony was not the same as being in school, the company was paying them, and until they started earning their salaries, they were a burden on the business.

He also compared working in a business to taking examinations: "If you do well on an exam and score 100%, that is fine, but if you don't write anything at all on your examination paper, you get a zero. In the world of business, you face an examination each day, and you gain not one hundred points but thousands of points, or only fifty points. But in business, if you make a mistake you do not get a simple zero. If you

Japan's high-speed bullet train, set against Mount Fuji. As technology advances, Sony, like other electronics companies, faces the growing challenge of moving with the times while respecting and improving the environment.

make a mistake, it is always minus something, and there is no limit to how far down you can go, so this could be a danger to the company."

Volunteers

Morita went on to describe the place of new employees in the company: "We did not draft you. This is not the army, so that means you have voluntarily chosen Sony. This is your responsibility, and normally if you join this company we expect that you will stay for the next twenty or thirty years." He told them to make it count, as the years spent at Sony could be the brightest time of their lives.

"When you leave the company ... I do not want you to regret that you spent all those years here. That would be a tragedy. I cannot stress the point too much that this is your responsibility to yourself," Morita said. "... the most important thing in the next few months is for you to decide whether you

"Sony seeks to maximize the individual's potential, to create a good working environment, and to ensure fair treatment for all."

From Sony and the New Europe.

49

will be happy or unhappy here. So even though we recruited you, we cannot ... make other people happy; happiness must be created yourself."

Cultural differences

Japanese attitudes to work differ from those of people in other countries. Akio Morita compared Western and Japanese companies to builders working with bricks and stones.

In the West, companies build as though they are working with bricks. The company plans everything well in advance and a complete framework for each job is decided. The company then advertises to find the person to fit the job exactly. Each part of the organization fits precisely into the plan – rather like a wall made from perfectly shaped bricks. In Japan, the best and most talented recruits are hired. The Japanese managers then have to decide how to use, and where to place, these strong, but unsorted, workers. This is rather like building a wall from

Opposite: Akio Morita was keen that his company should gain worldwide recognition – an achievement that was certainly realized. He remained actively involved with Sony until 1993 when he had to limit his duties for health reasons.

Below: Sony employees enjoy a day at the fair in celebration of the twenty-fifth anniversary of the founding of Sony (U.K.) Limited in May 1968. Sony as a company is keen to develop a sense of belonging among its workforce.

stone. Akio Morita said that people are like the pieces of stone; the "stones" are sometimes round, sometimes square, long, large, or small, but they are capable of being put together to make something strong and dependable. The Japanese realize that they have recruited the best, and if the business – the wall – needs to be changed then it will be possible to place their workers – the stones – in a different formation that becomes just as strong.

Rich, but not wealthy

This keenness to allow people to develop within the company is upheld by the Japanese idea of having a lifetime commitment to a business. This concept is often difficult for executives in other countries to understand. After the war, laws were put in place in Japan that made it difficult for workers to move from company to company. The World War II victors had been determined to prevent the Japanese from acquiring too much wealth and success too soon. This helped to establish the long term employment pattern.

Right for the job

In its work relations, Sony made very little distinction between a "blue-collar" worker and a "white-collar" one. A "blue-collar" worker is usually one who works in the factory, often doing a manual job. A "white-collar" worker is a member of the management team or the sales force. Management leaders are persuaders – they are chosen because they are good at talking and listening to people.

Sony did not believe in threatening or bullying anyone into working harder. It developed a policy over the years that allowed the company to match the right person with the right job within the organization. A person who joined Sony as a guard, might then apply for a job as a copywriter or secretary. If he or she had the ability to do the job – and the ambition – then that person would be moved accordingly. This is different from almost any other company – anywhere.

"Although company styles vary, what is certain is that all successful firms possess the ability to tap the potential of their employees so that people identify strongly with company goals and are willing to channel all their energies and enthusiasm into achieving them."

Rosemarie Stefanou, from
Understanding Industry Now.

Expansion

In the early days of Sony, Ibuka and Morita made the decision to make cassette tapes, and videotapes later, as well as the players and viewers. Their idea was that, having sold the hardware, there would be an automatic market for the software. The development and production of recording media became one of the main threads of the company's business. It was a natural step to become involved in putting music and film onto the tapes. To do this, Sony acquired a movie and record company.

In 1988 Sony bought the whole of CBS Records for $2 billion. In 1989 it acquired Columbia Pictures for $3.4 billion. As well as acquiring the rights to many great recording artists, the acquisition of CBS

Below: Having always been involved in music reproduction, Sony took the natural step of becoming involved in making the music itself. Sony Music Entertainment's stars include Mariah Carey and Michael Bolton.

Right: Musicians from the world of classical music and opera also work with Sony. The tenor Placido Domingo is well known for his vocal range.

Since acquiring its own movie company, Sony has enjoyed a string of successful movies, including Sleepless in Seattle, Howard's End, *and* My Life *(below) with stars Michael Keaton and Nicole Kidman.*

Records helped to introduce successfully the "MiniDisc." CBS Records was renamed Sony Music Entertainment and has continued to expand. The record label boasts stars such as Michael Bolton, Bruce Springsteen, Mariah Carey, and Sade. Its country music label leads the world with artists such as Mary Chapin-Carpenter and Dolly Parton.

Entertainment

The Sony Pictures Entertainment division has not only been responsible for many top movies such as *Sleepless in Seattle*, but also for pioneering technology to enhance film production. The Sony companies, Columbia and Tristar, have become established world leaders in both movie-making and home entertainment through video sales.

The movie business, however, is an unstable industry. As technology develops, so too do the costs of making pictures. If the movie does not recoup the costs through the box office, the movie company stands to lose. While Sony has had its successes, it has had to support some pictures that haven't made it.

Sony Pictures Entertainment has become associated with well-established stars such as Arnold Schwarzenegger, seen here in Last Action Hero.

Environmental issues

Sony also differed from other successful businesses by being aware that the world faces serious environmental problems. The depletion of the ozone layer, global warming, and the destruction of the world's rainforests are serious issues and the way many businesses are run often adds to these problems.

In October 1992, Sony began collecting nickel-cadmium rechargeable batteries through its 2,500 retail outlets in Japan. This rare material was then effectively recycled.

With worldwide growing concern for the environment, Sony's "Global Environmental Policy" was drawn up in 1993 to make every aspect of the company's operations more environmentally sound. This built on its efforts, begun in 1989, to phase out, as far as possible, the use of ozone-depleting substances in its production processes. It also brought in the use of recycled paper rather than a synthetic substance to make a pulp material for packing, and insisted upon only using cardboard cartons for the transportation of its products across the world. Sony Music Entertainment contributed to

The packaging around this camcorder and "Walkman" is made from pulp cushioning which is produced from recycled paper. Among their various commitments to environmental issues, Sony Music and Sony Pictures have recycled their equipment and actively supported environmental groups.

the cause by supporting organizations such as the Nature Conservancy and Rainforest Foundation. Sony Pictures also started recycling videotapes and wood used in the construction of sets for its movies and television shows.

A difficult balance

In Europe, Sony was the first Japanese company to participate in a joint research and development

One consequence of companies producing more and more new products in a throwaway society is the gradual build-up of waste that is environmentally damaging. Sony has shown its responsibility to the environment by taking steps to improve public awareness of this problem.

policy under the European Union's Environment project. The scheme focused on improving the recycling of consumer products. The relationship between business and the environment is one that is difficult to balance and so needs constantly revising. The president and chief executive officer of Sony, Norio Ohga, wrote in 1992, "We have to reconsider our corporate responsibilities, how we can repay the

community for our livelihood and the support it gives us, and we must strive even harder to take care of the environment and the world in which we and our company live."

Preservation and sponsorship

With Akio Morita's backing, Sony supported a huge range of educational, cultural, and medical causes. These included New York's Lincoln Center and the T. J. Martell Foundation for cancer and AIDS research. In Europe, Sony Italia S.p.A. sponsored the restoration of several monuments, including a statue of Leonardo da Vinci in Milan. In Japan, Sony gave grants for the promotion of science education from 1959 onwards.

A corporation founded by Sony and a Japanese welfare organization provided employment for people with physical disabilities. In Britain, Sony

Left: Through Sony's concern for the community, Sony Italia S.p.A. contributed to the costs of renovating the statue of Leonardo da Vinci in Milan.

Below: To help raise money for the Royal National Institute for the Blind, a Sony (U.K.) team took part in a sponsored cycle ride.

provided money to help children with cerebral palsy. And, to encourage its employees to be charitable and get involved in socially valuable activities in the different countries of the world, Sony also started a policy of matching any individual donation by one of its employees. It also gave time off to anyone taking part in volunteer work on the country's behalf.

Growth and development

By 1993 Sony Corporation employed 126,000 people across the world. Of these, 7% were top engineers and scientists who produced approximately one thousand new products a year. While 80% of the designs that were worked on involved the development of existing products, often using consumer feedback, the remaining 20% looked into developing new market areas. "Consumer electronics will continue to grow," Akio Morita

Sony's commitment to technology started early in the company's life and continues into the future. Here a camera and processor are used to accurately position electronic circuit boards.

revealed, "because we have many, many new applications of electronic technology for customers, not just for entertainment, but for household uses and in communications."

Innovation requires research and development. In the face of the rapid changes in technology, a company must invest in R & D in order to remain competitive and in business. To Akio Morita and Sony, commitment to innovation was crucial, and the key to becoming a main market leader in technology.

Retirement

Akio Morita provided much inspiration for the success of Sony Corporation. It was with great sadness, then, that on November 25, 1994, Mr. Morita resigned as chairman of the board and representative director, forty-eight years after founding the company. He had been unwell for some time and so the board respected his wishes and accepted his resignation with regret. In a statement, Norio Ohga reflected the whole company's regard for its founder, "I am sure that all of Sony's employees will do their very best to preserve and enhance the high regard in which Sony is held and which Mr. Morita helped to create."

"Ever since its foundation in 1946, Sony has considered itself to be an international enterprise which, although based in Japan, regards the entire world as its market-place."
From Sony and the New Europe.

Important dates

1921   Jan. 26: Akio Morita is born to Kyuzaemon and Shuko Morita in Kosugaya village, in Japan.

1940   At nineteen, Akio Morita takes up a place at Osaka Imperial University to study physics.

1942   Akio Morita works for several weeks in a factory making steel parts for Japanese planes.

1944   Akio Morita graduates from university with a degree in physics.

1945   As part of the war effort, Akio Morita is assigned to the office of Aviation Technology at Yokosuka, where he meets Masaru Ibuka.

1946   May 7: Akio Morita and Masaru Ibuka co-found an electronics company named Tokyo Tsushin Kogyo Kabushiki Kaisha (Tokyo Telecommunications Engineering Company).

1949   Akio Morita and Masaru Ibuka buy the shared rights to use a new high frequency system, AC-Bias.

1950   July: Toyko Telecommunications Engineering Company produces its first major consumer item, an audiotape recorder.

1951   Akio Morita marries Yoshiko Kamei.

1952   Akio and Yoshiko Morita's first son, Hideo, is born.

1953   Akio Morita travels to New York to buy the right to use transistors.

1954   A second son, Masao, is born to Akio and Yoshiko Morita.

1955   Aug.: The company's first transistor radio is sold.

1956   A daughter, Naoko, is born to Akio and Yoshiko Morita.

1958   Jan.: Tokyo Telecommunications Engineering Company officially changes its name to Sony Corporation.
Dec.: Sony is listed on the Tokyo Stock Exchange.

1960   Feb.: Sony Corporation of America is established, now Sony Electronics, Inc.
May: Sony launches the world's first transistor television.

1961   June: Sony's first research unit is opened.

1962   Sony opens its first store in the United States – on New York's Fifth Avenue.

1964   Akio Morita and his family move to the United States.

1968   Sony enters into a joint venture with the record company CBS, Inc.
May: Sony (U.K.) Limited is founded in Britain.
Oct.: The Trinitron television is launched by Sony.

1970	Sept.: Sony's shares are listed on the New York Stock Exchange.
1971	Akio Morita becomes president of Sony.
1975	May: "Betamax" home-use videotape recorders are launched.
1976	Akio Morita becomes chairman of Sony Corporation. Masaru Ibuka is made honorary chairman.
1979	Sony launches the first portable headphone stereo – "Walkman."
1982	Oct.: Sony markets the world's first compact-disc player.
1985	Sony launches the "Handycam" 8mm Camcorder.
1988	Jan.: Sony buys CBS Records, Inc., which becomes Sony Music Entertainment, Inc.
1989	Nov.: Sony buys Columbia Pictures Entertainment, Inc., which becomes Sony Pictures Entertainment.
1992	Nov.: The "MiniDisc" (MD) system is introduced by Sony.
1993	Sony draws up a "Global Environmental Policy" to make every aspect of the company's operations more environmentally sound. Sony employees around the world number 126,000.
1994	Nov. 25: Akio Morita resigns as chairman of the board and representative director of Sony Corporation, forty-eight years after founding the company.

Glossary

Amplifier: An electronic device used to increase the volume of sound running through the system.

Audiotape: A tape that reproduces sound mechanically, thus a tape to listen to.

Brand name: An identifying label, often the *company* name, given to a product which is immediately recognizable to the customer. Companies like to develop good reputations through branding, trying to convince customers that if they buy their brand, they are buying a quality *product.*

Chain store: One of a series of stores owned by the same person or *company,* all selling the same range of *products.*

Closed shop: A place of work where all workers are expected to belong to a specified *(trade) union.*

Compact Disc: A small disc that stores digital information. The *laser* beam decodes the information and changes it into sound signals that almost match the quality of the original sound.

Company or corporation: A group of two or more people that is registered to carry out a trade or business. A company is obliged to conform to certain regulations, which may vary from country to country or in the U.S., from state to state.

Consumer: A person who buys services or *products;* the customer.

Democracy: Government by the people, normally through elected representatives.

Executive: A person in a position of authority within a business or *company.*

Floppy disk: A device that stores information for computers on plates that have been coated with a magnetic layer.

High-frequency broadcasting transmission: The number of signals transmitted in a given time, resulting in a clearer signal with less noise interference.

Innovative: Having new and creative ideas.

Investment: When money, time or effort is put into something, i.e. setting up a business or buying a house, in the hope that it will result in a profit in the long-term.

Laser: A device used to concentrate light into a narrow beam. A laser beam can carry an immense amount of information - much more than a radio wave. Lasers are used in many areas of industry, including communications and medicine.

Manufacturer: A business or company responsible for the production of *products* on a large scale, usually using machinery.

Market: In terms of a *company*'s sales plan, the number of people who might want to buy a particular *product;* it also means to sell the *product* in an organized and preplanned way.

Microchip: A tiny piece of silicon containing many electrical circuits for use in electronic devices such as televisions and computers.

Ozone layer: A fragile layer, twelve to thirty miles (20–50 kms) above the earth's surface, made from an oxygen-related gas called ozone. It creates a protective layer, filtering ultraviolet rays from the sun before they reach the earth.

Pioneer: Someone who originates new ideas.

Product: An item that is either manufactured or naturally produced.

Prospectus: A printed pamphlet detailing the activities and achievements of a business.

Purchasing agent: A person who acts as a buyer on behalf of a company.

Recruitment: When new members are invited to join a *company.*

Royalty: A fee payable to the owner for the right to use a new invention.

Transistor: An electronic device that can strengthen a current or sound signal. Because it is very compact, it is used extensively in electronic equipment.

(Trade) Union: An association of workers from particular trades or professions that is formed to represent the workers' interests when negotiating with the employers.

Unit price: The price charged for each individual item, or unit, sold. Usually in business, the more individual items sold, the lower the unit price.

Index